FOOTBALL

THIS EDITION
Produced for DK by WonderLab Group LLC
Jennifer Emmett, Erica Green, Kate Hale, *Founders*

Editor Maya Myers; **Photography Editor** Nicole DiMella; **Managing Editor** Rachel Houghton;
Designers Project Design Company; **Researcher** Michelle Harris; **Copy Editor** Lori Merritt;
Indexer Connie Binder; **Proofreader** Susan K. Hom; **Series Reading Specialist** Dr Jennifer Albro

This edition published in 2025
First published in Great Britain in 2025 by
Dorling Kindersley Limited
20 Vauxhall Bridge Road,
London SW1V 2SA

The authorised representative in the EEA is
Dorling Kindersley Verlag GmbH. Arnulfstr. 124,
80636 Munich, Germany

Copyright © 2025 Dorling Kindersley Limited
10 9 8 7 6 5 4 3 2 1
001–345668–August/2025

All rights reserved.
Without limiting the rights under the copyright reserved above, no part of this publication may be reproduced, stored in or introduced into a retrieval system, or transmitted, in any form, or by any means (electronic, mechanical, photocopying, recording, or otherwise), without the prior written permission of the copyright owner.

DK values and supports copyright. Thank you for respecting intellectual property laws by not reproducing, scanning or distributing any part of this publication by any means without permission. By purchasing an authorised edition, you are supporting writers and artists and enabling DK to continue to publish books that inform and inspire readers. No part of this publication may be used or reproduced in any manner for the purpose of training artificial intelligence technologies or systems. In accordance with Article 4(3) of the DSM Directive 2019/790, DK expressly reserves this work from the text and data mining exception.

Published in Great Britain by Dorling Kindersley Limited

A CIP catalogue record for this book
is available from the British Library.
ISBN: 978-0-2417-2383-8

Printed and bound in China

Super Readers Lexile® levels 620L to 790L
Lexile® is the registered trademark of MetaMetrics, Inc. Copyright © 2024 MetaMetrics, Inc. All rights reserved.

The publisher would like to thank the following for their kind permission to reproduce their images:
a=above; c=centre; b=below; l=left; r=right; t=top; b/g=background
Alamy Stock Photo: Aflo Co. Ltd. / Nippon News 8, Allstar Picture Library Ltd 30, 31, 36cl, Associated Press / Jason Mowry / Icon Sportswire 3, CPA Media Pte Ltd / Pictures From History 16bl, DPA Picture Alliance 44tl, imageBROKER.com GmbH & Co. KG 10b, PA Images / David Davies 39bl, PA Images / Empics 20-21b, PA Images / Laurence Griffiths 25, Sipa US / Oliver Contreras 35tr, ZUMA Press, Inc. 40tr; **Bridgeman Images:** © National Football Museum 16tr, 17tr; **Dreamstime:** Natthaphong Janpum 40-41, Worakit Sirijinda 38-39; **Getty Images:** AFP / Paul Ellis 38t, AFP / Pierre-Philippe Marcou 1, Naomi Baker 27, Bob Thomas Sports Photography / Bob Thomas 21tr, 22, 23, Steph Chambers 41t, Stanley Chou 20cl, Stephen Dunn 19tc, Eurasia Sport Images 10tl, 40bl, 43, FIFA / Maja Hitij 9, El Grafico 29, Laurence Griffiths 37, Matthias Hangst 45, Richard Heathcote 7, 14, Harry How 13t, Hulton Archive 28bl, Catherine Ivill 12, Alika Jenner 34-35, Alexandre Loureiro 18cr, Matt McNulty 44tr, Buda Mendes 11, Mirrorpix 28br, Dan Mullan 6, 13b, NurPhoto 15, 42br, Bob Thomas / Popperfoto 18tl, Paul Popper / Popperfoto 17bl, Popperfoto 19, 33b, Popperfoto / Professional Sport 24, Rolls Press / Popperfoto 32-33, Power Sport Images 42tl, Clive Rose 39br, Jamie Squire 36, UEFA / Sarah Stier 26; **Shutterstock.com:** Katatonia82 4-5

Cover images: *Front:* **Alamy Stock Photo:** Mark Pain bl, Sportimage Ltd cl, ZUMA Press, Inc. c; **Dreamstime.com:** Photolight (Background); **Getty Images:** Diego Souto br; *Back:* **Dreamstime.com:** Bigmouse108

www.dk.com

This book was made with Forest Stewardship Council™ certified paper — one small step in DK's commitment to a sustainable future.
Learn more at www.dk.com/uk/information/sustainability

Level 3

FOOTBALL

Emma Carlson Berne

Contents

6   A Beautiful Game
8   On the Pitch
16 Passion to Play
22 Moments to Remember
32 World's Greatest

42 The Future on the Pitch
46 Glossary
47 Index
48 Quiz

A Beautiful Game

Almost 90,000 fans packed into the stadium to watch the 2022 World Cup final. The reigning World Cup champion team, France, was about to face off with Argentina. For the last 29 days, football was all anyone could talk about. Lionel Messi of Argentina had played in 26 matches and was now chasing the trophy. Morocco had become the first African nation to make it to a semi-final. Then, the game began.

The two teams battled through the first half. At 23 minutes, Messi put Argentina on the scoreboard with a penalty kick. His team-mate, Ángel Di María, added to their score in the 36th minute. Argentina dominated the game from there. With under 10 minutes to go in normal time, Kylian Mbappé of France scored twice. The game was tied at 2–2. Messi scored again. Mbappé scored again. The game went to extra time and then to a penalty shootout.

Kylian Mbappé

   After almost three hours, six goals and eight penalty kicks, Argentina won. Messi got his trophy. Fans around the world remembered that the game is never decided until the final whistle.

On the Pitch

Football is the world's most popular sport. It is played in nearly every country on Earth! Some countries refer to the game as football and some refer to it as soccer.

Professional football players play for clubs. Many clubs have men's, women's and youth teams. These clubs compete in leagues based in their country. Around the world, some of the leagues are the Premier League in England, Serie A in Italy and LaLiga in Spain. Some players are chosen to play for their national teams, too. These teams compete in friendly international matches or in international tournaments, such as the World Cup.

Football is played on a flat field known as a pitch. Players try to kick the ball into the goals. Each team can have 11 players on the pitch at most. Games are played in two 45-minute halves. Stoppage time is when the players have stopped but the clock keeps running. This time is added on to the end of a half.

The goalkeeper stands in front of the net and tries to stop the ball from going in. Goalies often wear gloves and a different-coloured kit from the rest of the team. One reason is so the referees can see them more easily.

The defenders stand near the goalie. They are the last chance to block the ball before it reaches the goalie.

Midfielders
Midfielders have to be able to run long distances. During one game, a midfielder might run between 8 and 12 kilometres.

The midfielders are the bridge between defence and attack. They try to move the ball from the back line up to the front line.

The attackers, or forwards, play closest to the other team's goal. The striker is the forward in the middle. They are the main scoring player on a team. The other forwards try to score goals, too. They also pass to the striker so the striker can score.

Shootout

A shootout is what happens when a tournament game ends in a tie. Players take turns taking penalty kicks at the goal. The team that scores the most penalty kicks out of five wins.

If a player kicks the ball and it goes into the net, their team has scored a goal. To win the game, a team has to score more goals than the other team.

If a player gets fouled, the referee might award them a penalty kick. The foul has to happen in the opposing team's penalty area. When there is a penalty kick, the player gets to take one free shot at the goal. Only the goalie can block the ball.

If the ball goes off the side of the pitch, a player will get a throw-in. If the ball goes off either end of the pitch, either a corner kick or a goal kick is awarded.

Foul Play
Players who foul other players might get a yellow card. This card is a warning. A red card means the player is sent off and cannot finish the game.

Assists are a key part of the game. These are passes to another player who then scores a goal. Headers are another way to get the ball into the net. Players might also bounce the ball off their chests.

Strikers usually try to get the ball as close as they can to the goal. They will point their non-kicking foot in the direction they want to shoot. Then, they'll kick with the top of their foot, where the laces of the shoe are. This makes the ball fly faster and with more power.

Passion to Play

Eight-paneled leather football with lacing, c. 1912–14

For more than 2,000 years, people have been kicking round objects for fun. Archaeologists studying ancient China and Greece have found balls of rock or leather stuffed with hair. During the medieval period, Europeans kicked an animal bladder stuffed with dried peas. They also used a leather bag stuffed with rags. Whole villages played against each other. Sometimes, the goals would be miles apart!

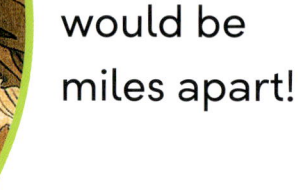

Painting of children at play with a ball

Modern football first started in the 19th century. Boys in British boarding schools played against each other. In 1863, the first football association was formed. The rules for the game were written down as well. Football spread around the world. New migrants from Europe took the game to the United States.

Men's football appeared at the Olympics for the first time in 1900. But it wasn't an official Olympic sport until 1908, when seven countries sent players. More and more countries added teams during each Games. By 1924, 23 countries sent teams to play in the Paris Games.

Women's football wasn't added to the Olympics until 1996. Only eight countries sent teams.

Paralympics
Paralympic athletes began playing Paralympic football in 1984. Teams usually have seven players on a side instead of 11. In 2016 after the Rio Games, officials worried that players weren't being properly trained and prepared. Seven-a-side Paralympic football was dropped. However, five-a-side football for blind Paralympic athletes remained.

So many countries were playing football that the athletes needed an international organisation. In the early 1900s, the International Federation of Association Football, known as FIFA, was created. FIFA is the governing body of international football.

FIFA organised the globe's first international football tournament, the World Cup, in 1930. Thirteen men's teams travelled to Uruguay in South America to compete. The host nation, Uruguay, won.

1930 World Cup final game, Uruguay v. Argentina

Since then, the men's World Cup has been held every four years except during World War II and the Covid-19 pandemic.

The first official Women's World Cup was held in China in 1991. In the final game, 65,000 fans were in the stadium as the United States beat Norway.

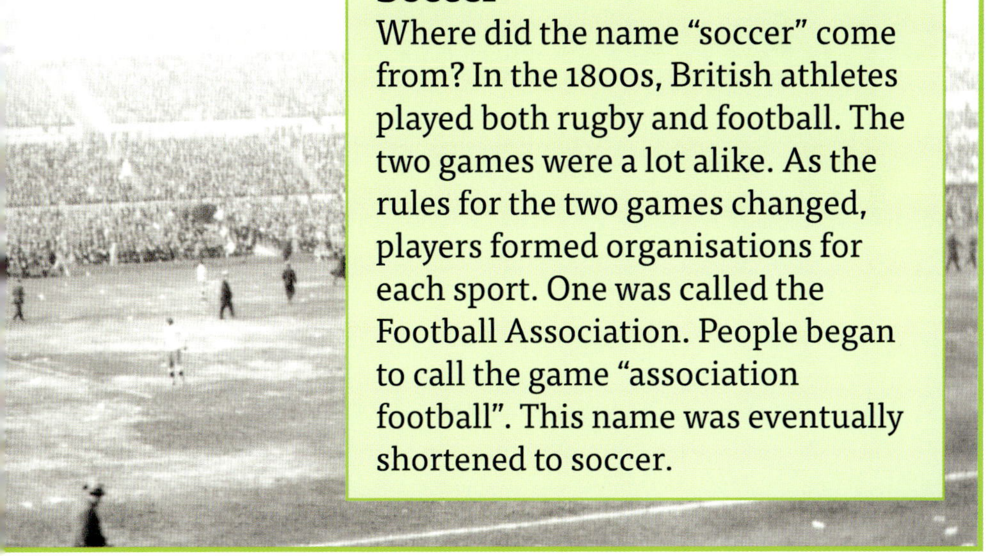

Soccer
Where did the name "soccer" come from? In the 1800s, British athletes played both rugby and football. The two games were a lot alike. As the rules for the two games changed, players formed organisations for each sport. One was called the Football Association. People began to call the game "association football". This name was eventually shortened to soccer.

Julie Foudy beats Wen Sun to the ball.

Moments to Remember

Football has offered some of the greatest moments in sports history. Countries and players from around the world have awed audiences at home and on the world's stage. Here are just a few of the biggest games of all time.

1996 USWNT (US Women's National Team)

In 1996, women's football was introduced to the Olympic Games. The US Women's National Team was led by stars Brandi Chastain, Mia Hamm and Julie Foudy. They beat Denmark, Sweden and Norway to play in the gold medal match.

The final game against China drew the largest crowd to watch a women's sports event at that time. Forward Tiffeny Milbrett slammed the ball into the goal for the win.

The players all stepped onto the podium together to accept their gold medals.

This historic win led to the rise in popularity in women's football and women's sports in the United States.

Michelle Akers with a gold medal

Beckham Is the Best in the League

The English Premier League is one of the best leagues in the world. The league began in 1992 when the top teams separated into their own league. The worst teams would be relegated, or moved down a level. Twenty teams compete against each other. They win points to see who will be the best in the league.

In 1996, the reigning champions, Manchester United, took to the pitch. It was opening day for the league. Manchester United took a 2–0 lead over Wimbledon. Then, David Beckham got the ball. He was only 21 years old and had not yet made a name for himself. Everything changed that day.

Beckham was on his side of the pitch. He raced forward with the ball. Then, he saw the goalkeeper on the other side out of position. He took a shot. The ball sailed from midfield over the goalkeeper's head. Beckham had scored from his own side of the pitch! Manchester United won the game. David Beckham became one of the most well-known players in the world.

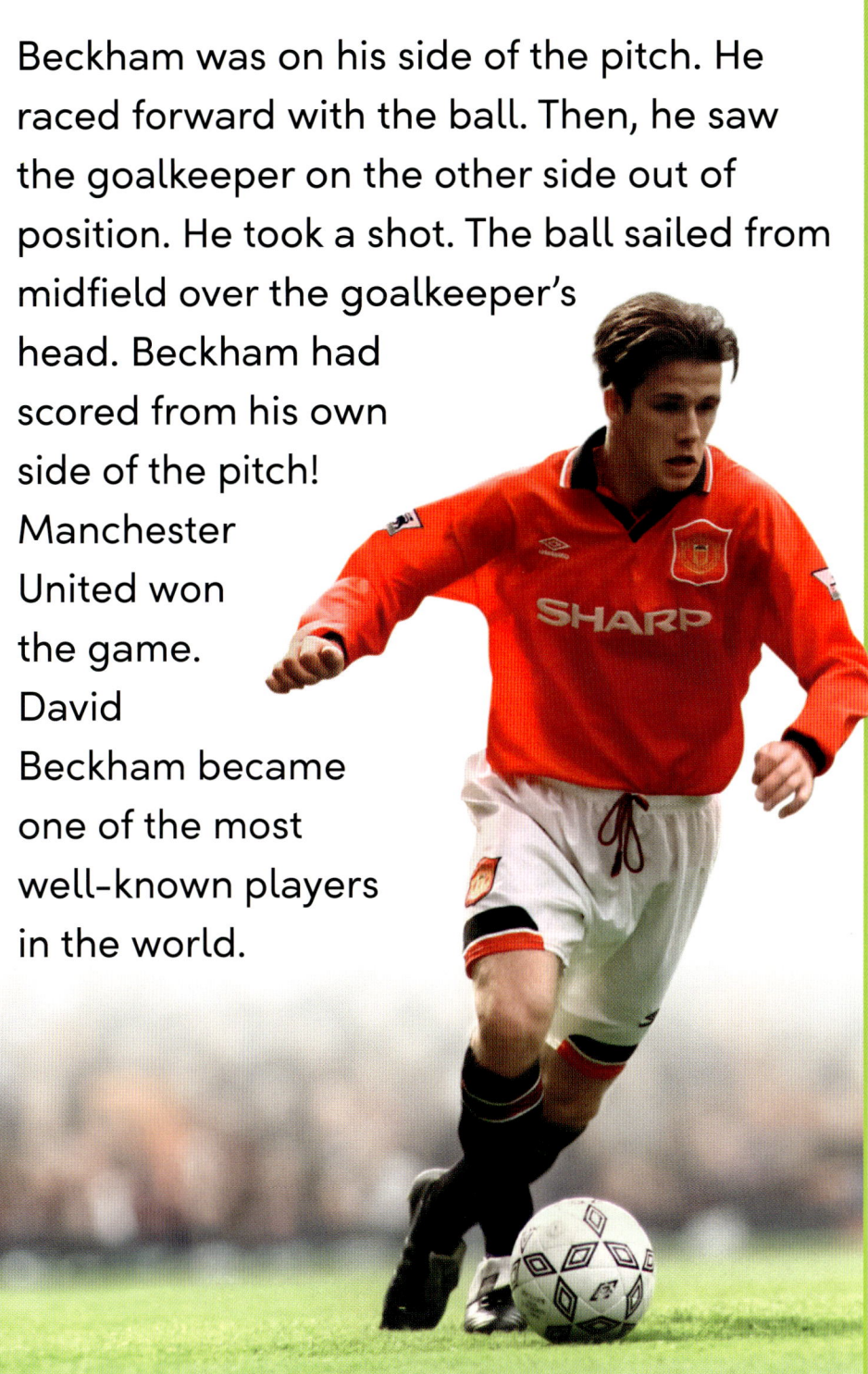

Lionesses Roar

The crowd that packed into England's Wembley Stadium on 31 July, 2022, was the biggest ever for a women's European Championship game. England faced off against Germany.

It was a competitive match from the start. English forward, Ellen White, had the first shot on Germany's goal. She missed. Germany responded with a shot on England's goal but it was blocked. The teams battled it out through the first half. They went to their changing rooms scoreless.

Around ten minutes into the second half England brought on forward Ella Toone. Seven minutes later, Toone was the sole forward racing towards Germany's side of the pitch. She took her shot. The ball sailed into the net.

Germany tied the game. When normal time ended, the score was 1–1.

England's Chloe Kelly scored again in extra time. And when the clock stopped, England had won 2–1. It was the first win for either England's men or women since 1966.

Hand of God

All eyes were on the 1986 World Cup quarter-final match between Argentina and England. The two teams had been rivals since the 1960s.

Argentina's Diego Maradona scored two goals for the team. But it is Maradona's first goal against England that still makes headlines.

The first half of the game was scoreless. Six minutes into the second half, Maradona saw a break in the action. He headed towards England's goal ready for a pass from his team-mate. The ball soared through the air. England's goalie came out of the goal to knock the ball away. But Maradona was in the air. He connected with the ball and sent it into the net. He said he scored the goal with his head and the hand of God. England protested. They said he hit the ball into the net with his hand.

Argentina won the game and the trophy. But years later, there are still questions over whether the ball hit Maradona's hand.

Miracle of Istanbul

Liverpool was down 3–0 in the 2005 Union of European Football Associations (UEFA) final game. Milan had scored in the first minute of the match. Then, two more times. At half-time, it looked like Liverpool's chances were slim.

Liverpool made some changes to the lineup when they came back onto the pitch. Captain Steven Gerrard scored first. He sent a header into the net to make the score 3–1. Liverpool scored again. Then, six minutes after their first goal of the game, the score was tied 3–3. The game went to extra time, then penalty kicks. After nine kicks, four for Liverpool and five for Milan, Liverpool came out on top. It was one of the greatest comebacks in history.

World's Greatest

Pelé

Brazilian football player Pelé was one the best-known athletes in the world. He was born in 1940 to a poor family. Pelé used to kick a grapefruit around because he didn't have a football. But at the age of 16, Pelé exploded onto the world football scene. He was a powerful kicker. He could also predict the movements of players on the other team. Pelé was a astonishingly fast, creative, graceful player. He went on to win three World Cups, the most of any player. He is also still the youngest player to ever win a World Cup. He eventually scored over 1,200 goals in his career before his death in 2022.

Megan Rapinoe

Megan Rapinoe played on the boys' football team when she was growing up. There were no girls' football teams where she lived. She and her sister learned to play by following their older brother.

Megan played football for the University of Portland. She joined the US Women's National Team in 2006. She helped lead the USWNT to Olympic gold and bronze medals. She also won two World Cups.

Megan has been a powerful voice for social issues, speaking out for LGBTQ rights and for racial and gender equality. In 2022, Megan was awarded the Presidential Medal of Freedom. US President Joe Biden wanted to recognise her for her work helping others.

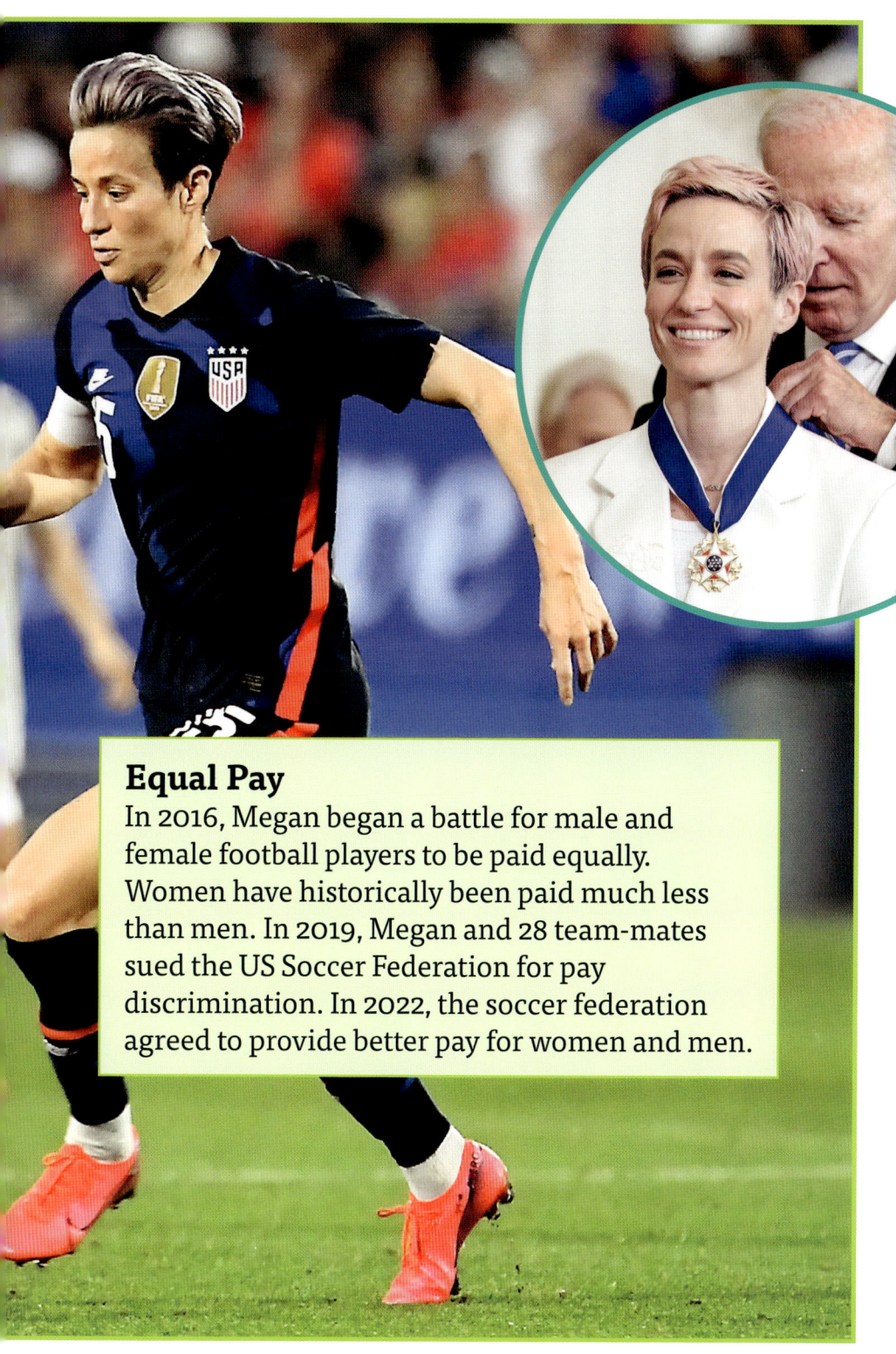

Equal Pay

In 2016, Megan began a battle for male and female football players to be paid equally. Women have historically been paid much less than men. In 2019, Megan and 28 team-mates sued the US Soccer Federation for pay discrimination. In 2022, the soccer federation agreed to provide better pay for women and men.

Lionel Messi

Lionel Messi was born in 1987 in Rosario, Argentina. When he was eight, Messi started playing football with his older brothers. He was an extraordinary dribbler. His coaches remembered later that he seemed to have a magnet attached to his boots. Messi was also very small for his age. It didn't stop him from becoming one of the best football players in the world, though.

Lionel joined the legendary FC Barcelona men's team when he was a teenager. He played for the Spanish club for 17 seasons. He eventually became one of the most decorated players in football history.

Aitana Bonmatí Conca

Spain's Aitana Bonmatí Conca is one of the best players in women's football. She started playing at the age of seven and joined FC Barcelona's women's team as a teenager. She played in their youth side before moving up in 2016. She made history with the team when they won their first UEFA Championship in May 2021. She did it again in 2023 when she led the team to Spain's first World Cup title.

Alisson Becker

Brazilian football player Alisson Becker is one of the best goalies on the planet. As a player for English club Liverpool FC, he helped Liverpool win two league championships during his first two seasons with the club. He also helped the Brazilian National Team win championships in 2019. Alisson is known for being just as quick to stop a ball with his feet as he is with his hands.

Marta

Many people think of the Brazilian player Marta as the greatest female football player of all time. Marta has played in six World Cups. She was Player of the Year six times. This is more than any other female player. Marta is Brazil's all-time top goal scorer for men and women. She scored 119 goals in her career.

Abderrazak Hattab

Born in Morocco, Abderrazak Hattab is the Paralympic champion in blind football. In 2016, he helped Morocco to become the first African blind football team to appear at a Paralympic Games. He then scored the first goal ever for Morocco. Hattab kept up his streak, leading his team to a bronze medal at the 2020 Paralympics.

The Future on the Pitch

Football continues to grow around the world. Most of the successful football players and teams have come from Europe and South America. But teams in North America, Africa and Asia are hoping to compete with these other continents. The number of teams in international tournaments has grown with each event. With this rise in talent around the world, the world's major tournaments will become even more exciting.

Women's football continues to become more popular around the world as well. Twice the amount of people watched the 2023 Women's World Cup as watched the 2019 tournament. Players are hoping that more fans will also mean better pay and better training for the teams. They also hope to see more women moving into leadership roles in football organisations.

Updated technology is also making its way into games. The Video Assistant Referee, or VAR, system has been used to help game officials make decisions. A team of three people watch different angles of the game in real time on screens. They are able to recommend changes to decisions made on the pitch. Some leagues are rethinking how they want to use technology in the game, though. They believe the system has changed the game. The VAR reviews have slowed down play in some cases. They have also overturned goals in very close calls.

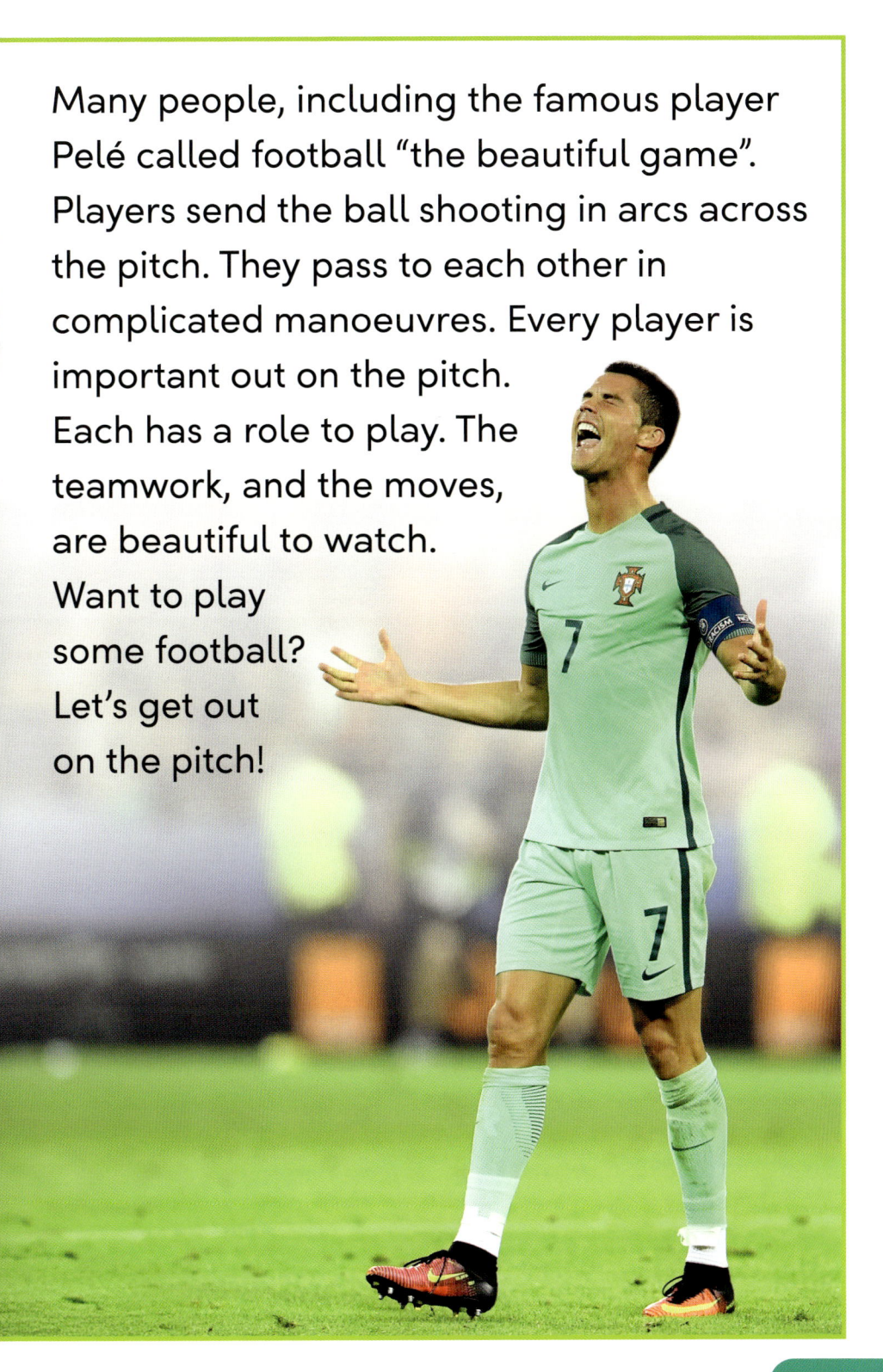

Many people, including the famous player Pelé called football "the beautiful game". Players send the ball shooting in arcs across the pitch. They pass to each other in complicated manoeuvres. Every player is important out on the pitch. Each has a role to play. The teamwork, and the moves, are beautiful to watch. Want to play some football? Let's get out on the pitch!

Glossary

Association
A group organised for a particular purpose

Decorated
Awarded honours or medals

Equality
A state of being equal, especially in status or rights

Football club
A sports club that organises their team and games within a league

Fouled
Committed an unfair act in a sport

Immigrants
People who have travelled to a country other than the one they were born in, in order to live

International
Between different countries

Leagues
A group of sports teams that regularly play each other

Manoeuvres
Skilful movements

Medieval
The period of time from approximately 476 CE to 1400 CE

Paralympics
International contests for athletes with disabilities held after the Olympics

Penalty
A punishment against a team or a player for breaking a rule

Podium
A raised area where a person can stand to receive a medal

Tournament
A sports competition in which a series of games are played and the winners of each game play each other

Stoppage time
A period of time when play was stopped that is added to the end of a half

Index

Akers, Michelle 23
Argentina 6–7, 28–29, 37
assists 14
attackers 11
ball 16
Becker, Alisson 39
Beckham, David 24–25
Biden, Joe 34, 35
blind football 18, 41
Bonmatí Conca, Aitana 38
Brazil 33, 39, 40, 45
Chastain, Brandi 23
China 21, 23
clubs 8
corner kick 13
defenders 10, 11
Denmark 23
Di María, Ángel 7
England 8, 24–29, 39
equal pay 35
FC Barcelona 37, 38
FIFA (International Federation of Association Football) 20; see also World Cup
forwards 11
Foudy, Julie 22, 23
foul play 13
France 6–7

future of football 42–44
Germany 26–27
Gerrard, Steven 31
goalkeeper (goalie) 10, 13
goal kick 13
Hamm, Mia 23
Hattab, Abderrazak 41
headers 14
history 16–21
Italy 8
Kelly, Chloe 27
LaLiga (Spain) 8
Liverpool FC 30–31, 39
Manchester United 24–25
Maradona, Diego 28–29
Marta 40
Mbappé, Kylian 7
Messi, Lionel 6–7, 37
midfielders 11
Milan 30–31
Milbrett, Tiffeny 23
Morocco 6, 41
Norway 21, 23
Olympics 18, 23, 34
Paralympics 18, 41
Pelé 33, 45
penalty kicks 7, 12, 13

pitch 9, 13
players
 number of 9, 18
 positions 10–11
Premier League (England) 8, 24–25
Rapinoe, Megan 34–35
red card 13
referee 13
Serie A (Italy) 8
shootout 12
Spain 8, 38
stoppage time 9
strikers 11, 15
Sweden 23
throw-in 13
Toone, Ella 27
Union of European Football Associations (UEFA) 30–31, 38
United States 21, 23, 34
Uruguay 20
Video Assistant Referee (VAR) 44
Wen Sun 22
White, Ellen 26
Wimbledon 24–25
Women's World Cup 21, 34, 38, 40, 43
World Cup 6–7, 20, 28–29, 33
yellow card 13

47

Quiz

Answer the questions to see what you have learned. Check your answers in the key below.

1. What might a player be awarded if someone commits a foul against them?
2. What position is the bridge between the forwards and the defence?
3. True or false: Blind football is a Paralympic sport.
4. What did medieval football players sometimes use for a ball?
5. True or false: The striker is the only player on the pitch who can touch the ball with their hands.

1. Penalty kick 2. The midfielders 3. True 4. Animal bladders or leather bags stuffed with animal hair or rags 5. False: The goalie is the only player on the pitch who can touch the ball with their hands.